Star Apple Blue and Avocado Green

Star Apple
Blue and
Avocado
Green

Poems by
Paulette A. Ramsay

IAN RANDLE PUBLISHERS
Kingston • Miami

First published in Jamaica, 2016 by
Ian Randle Publishers
16 Herb McKenley Drive
Box 686
Kingston 6
www.ianrandlepublishers.com

© 2016 Paulette A. Ramsay
ISBN 978-976-637-918-6 (pbk)

National Library of Jamaica Cataloguing-in-Publication Data

Ramsay, Paulette.

     Star apple blue and avocado green / Paulette A. Ramsay.

pages. ; cm.

ISBN 978-976-637-918-6

1. Jamaican poetry   2. Jamaican literature

811 – dc 23

Cover image © Aiesha Panton. Used with permission of the artist.
Cover and Book Design by Ian Randle Publishers
Printed and Bound in the United States of America

Contents

Acknowledgements

Many thanks to Trudy, Peta-Gaye, Tamika and especially to Sharon Clue for their help in different ways with this manuscript. Once again, I thank Prof. Edward Baugh for taking the time to read many of the poems and for giving me useful feedback. I thank Carol Bailey for reading the poems and giving me very useful comments, despite her many pressing commitments. Many thanks to Curdella Forbes, for listening, reading, laughing, critiquing and giving great suggestions as usual. I thank all those who continue to encourage me to just write on....

Closing Doors

Closing Doors

a young woman sits on the edge
of a four poster bed in the five star hotel
in the Dominican Republic
a battered bank book
quietly peeps at her from the top
of her expensive leather handbag

she watches as the sun sets
beyond the placid purple blue waves
of the Caribbean Sea
the Malecón is inviting in the quiet dark,
six limp leather suitcases
patiently wait on the marble floor
announcing the end of an arduous journey,
a long way
from the tiny ramshackle in Jamaica
where it all began,
when three bank accounts
were impossible dreams

a long way from the grip of poverty
and the unrelenting teeth of hunger
gnawing at the walls of her stomach,
driving her to seek refuge
in the beds of wealthy old men
with breaths smelling of stale tobacco
and fiery Caribbean rum,

She cautiously takes the bank book
from her aged leather handbag, smells it slowly
mindfully checks the numbers again
slowly returns it to its safe place
deep inside her silk brassiere,
she smiles wistfully at the foaming purple blue
and avocado green waves
her colours of laughter and life
and continues to sip her cup of tepid red tea.

Star Apple Blue and Avocado Green

our star apple tree is old and tired now
so many many years after my
great grandmother planted it
it now leans lazily yet gracefully
against the avocado tree that I planted
ten years ago
interestingly, they each carry stories
of two different generations
in a family that celebrates
our tropical trees with great spirit
my great grandmother loved the star apple's purple blue skin
and its succulent purple and white flesh
so delicately arranged in a wine coloured bowl
I planted my avocado for its smooth, waxy fruit
that my mother used to feed me
with hot slices of yellow heart roasted breadfruit
they seem to like each other's company
my avocado tree seems happy to
bear the weight of my great grandmother's
aged star apple tree with its purple green leaves

the star apple tree is happy to find
friendly support in a young strong trunk
in its last days
so reminiscent of the way great grandmother
loved the company of us young people
as we laughed and chattered around her
in her last days

our two trees seem to like
the cosiness of being snuggled against each other
listening to the soft whisper of their leaves
brushing against each other
in the quiet green breeze

sometimes I watch them with envy
I contemplate joining them
but then I wonder
who will I lean on
my avocado, or great grandmother's star apple?
for now, I'm content to just watch them
or close my eyes and imagine myself
sitting in the V where they meet
surrounded by star apple blue and avocado green
flowers and colours, my colours of life and joy.

Potiphar's Wife

The first time
Joseph saw his neighbour Potiphar's wife
crouched against his semi-transparent hedge,
pulling up invisible weeds,
making onomatopoeia with her mouth
and snake-like contortions with her sleek body
he built a long steel fence
around his yard,
sprinkled old time repellents
along its length and breadth
then sat down
and planted crimson flowers
with militant *maccas*
along its length and breadth,
all the time
making onomatopoeia
with his own mouth.

An Angry Woman Speaks to Her Body of Corpulence

so you have I notice
resolved to defy me
not to yield one ounce
of obdurate lard,
despite days of flagellation
months of climbing
treacherous mountains
you insist on hanging on
to every dangling part
every tightly rolled
ball of lard

I can hardly not notice,
it's truly outrageous,

I'm amazed at this,

as unbelievable as it is,

forget appeals to pathos
forget appeals to logic
you remain
an artistic menace
but be warned that today,
without success
the size six purple-blue frock mocks me still
but I promise you,
you will shrink,
to near obscurity...
one day.

I jump and twist

it is a sure threat,
I can visualise it,

The Way She Was

rolled up tightly in a ball
cold and hard
like the metal on a well-built railway line,
daunting like Miss Clara James' cactus hedge,
afraid of her silhouette
afraid of her own reflection in the mirror
afraid of everyone, especially herself

then one day
the sun slid smoothly
from beneath thick cumulus clouds
in her head,
the entire galaxy
all the purple blue waves of the Caribbean Sea and beyond
activated to the reggae beat
stifled in her head, through self-denying rites
and everyday rhythm became beautiful
and invigorating.

Now she smiles wistfully at butterflies
laughs at busy birds pecking at Julie mangoes
dances to Negro spirituals
hallelujah choruses
and conscious reggae rhythms
all the time
laughing with herself
laughing with the world,
making her own syncopated sounds
wondering why for so long
she refused to live.

I Learned to Dance

I learned to dance
to trample sorrow under feet

I learned to dance
so I could toss my head back
and move my shoulders and hips
to rhythms of freedom and joy

I learned to dance
to watch my body twirl and twist
with rhythmic ease

I learned to dance
so laughter would escape
from my mouth
as my body and soul
would glide upon the wings of rhythm

I learned to dance
so that my feet can join my hands and clap
together with the hills
leap, prance through the air

and I learned to dance, so you could see
that I love me, love to feel the cool green air
against my face
and that together me, my body and mind
have found rhythm and joy.

(Un)like Lot's Wife

like Lot's wife
I turned into a pillar of salt
understood the error
of looking back;
(un)like Lot's wife
I melted slowly
and survived
on the salt
of my molten tears.

I Have Loved and Lost

many things,
in many different ways,
my grandmother's antiquated wooden house
eaten to the ground by pitiless termites,
my innocent village
over-run by uninvited strangers
with no love in their hearts, no love
for our breadfruit trees
our star-apples and hog plums,
our unsophisticated old people, simple and sincere
our parochial young children.

I've loved and lost
a house that still carries the echo of my voice
decorated with the delicate strings of my heart
I've loved and lost
my favourite avocado green shoes, pliable leather
that made me sympathise
with the bovine that surrendered its life
just for my feet
carried off by yesterday's flood waters
that sucked them from my soles
clapping as they skipped away with them, thieving waters.
It's a truth most people now believe
that one day they will lose everything
especially what they love most
while the world will continue
to breathe, live and laugh.

Reflections on the Dirty Dishes in the Sink
(For Heather Bowie)

I do not own
the dirty dishes in the sink
they really do not belong to me
they certainly are not part
of some special collection
of dirty things that I own.

I sometimes explain
to myself, to the air
to those who listen to me
that of the ten dirty cups in the sink
my DNA can be found on one
and on one fork, one knife
and perhaps a tiny teaspoon,
do not expect then to be praised
each time you wash the dishes
and please, I beg of you
do not wash the dishes
as a special favour to me

do not think of me
as the lucky beneficiary
of your thoughtfulness
just do the dishes because you care
about keeping the world
free from your germs.
Or perhaps, because you need them clean
for the next time you need to eat or drink.

The Rats Come out at Nights

right after she puts her children to bed
they move stealthily, like cowardly thieves
and feverishly nibble at the dried bread
she feeds her children for supper
she will use her bare hands
to smother the life
out of them
if she but catches them
trying to steal to live, spread diseases
and disturb her children's sleep
or even the *siesta* of her indolent cats.

Beijing Salute

Me
black woman in China
I feel eyes x-ray me
Someone, curious, pulls my coarse hair, surprised
it does not separate from my scalp,
a woman, skeptical, touches my skin, surprised,
its black does not rub off,
and stain her hands
someone speaks to me
hello Africa
hello China, I say
we smile together,
we are people together,
me, Caribbean woman
she, Beijing woman.

(Re)making Self

no stones
no blocks
no steel
just woman will
spiritual reconnection
with Mother earth
communion with the Almighty,
inevitable in this mess

reflection, on how they define me
rejection, of how they define me
self-rewrite
remade woman of pride
moving my unaggressive face
into everybody's space
silencing the myth-makers.

Luna Mystery

nobody ever spoke
the truth
there is a woman in the moon
una mujer en la luna
just a man and his dog
they always say,
just imagine
the world being like
that moon.

Naissance

of your indifference
I do not know...
of your hatred
I cannot rationalize
naissance
of your self-centredness
I will never fathom
or your deeply entrenched sexism
I will never accept.

The Girl with the Big Heart

hers is a heart
not unused to being broken apart
by many a dart
even from the arrows
of treacherous lovers
not one to take cover, or cower
she takes the blows
one by one,
and quietly keeps count
for she knows, without doubt
that time and pain
will both bring gain
mend her heart
set her apart
from those who are meek
faint-hearted and weak.

The Reason She Sings

she can read her own letter now
no more running to the fence
to beg Miss Mary or Mass Harold
or the little ten year boy old across the road
to tell her what her sister
in America write to tell her

hallelujah!
she's discovered the gift of literacy
thanks to some people
who looked her in the eyes
told her to stop pretending
and taught her how to use
a, e, i, o, u, to make sounds
that make words and sentences
and made an honest woman of her

no more pretending
to be reading from the hymnal, on Sundays
no more twist up twist up mouth
to try to sing the same words
as Pastor, the choir and everybody else
every magazine in the doctor's office
every book on her own likkle bookshelf
bought for show, mere adornment
now screams at her
and she can tell what they all say

no more pretending her eye is dark
no more pretending she is hoarse
she can sing in her best soprano
the gift of words
the gift of the Word
the gift of reading, is the reason she sings,
hallelujah, hallelujah!

No Memories Great Enough to Keep Me Here

on Friday morning when Caleb received word
that his Adina had passed
he announced in that weary, vacant voice
that came from the faraway place
he retreated to the day Adina fell gravely ill,

"After sixty-three years, she gone,
I not staying,
not staying in this place
with no memories great enough to keep me
sitting and dreaming of the way she used to be."

So on Sunday morning
he closed his eyes
and willed himself to take flight
over the restless waves of the air and sea
to find her, along with the best memories
she had carried with her,
to that place with purple blue
and avocado green lights.

Speaking in Halves

Oxymoron

a black woman with Indian gold weave
the little black girl with her lily white doll
pressed closely against her cheek
you, trying to silence me

a dreadlock priest
serving communion
in a six o'clock mass
me and you
a Putin and Obama embrace

a fierce sunshine at midnight
while we toss and turn
on expensive sheets
on uncomfortable mattresses

a green card holder
in the visitor's line today
at Norman Manley International Airport
in front of me
eyeing me with pity

the same green
card holder behind me
in the visitor's line next month
in Miami International Airport
smiling at me
with great empathy.

Speaking in Halves

have you ever noticed how these days
I speak in halves
half a sentence
half a word
half a thought
even half a syllable

it's my mind you see,
beginning to remember in halves
forgetting in halves
I dread the thought
of remembering nothing,
forgetting all

if you listen
you will realise
I remember only half
your name
you'd be surprised
if I told you
I remember only half your face
I call my child by half his name
you, Em, I say for Emanuel
you, Pe, I say for what they
say is Petunia

And now I'm beginning
to wonder
how much of me
do I really remember
all, or half
and if only a half,
which half ...

Jordan Crossing

after the *dénouement* of this obscure myth
this postmodern *guerra*
when I stand on the brink
of swiftly gushing waters
dreading the arrival of the river

who will part the waters,
who will leave a path
straight and narrow
for me;
should I look for
Charon with his ominous boat,
or believe that quiet, distant whisper
that the Moses
of Judah is still alive?

fallen angel
on the run
sin shame
sin remorse
sin redención

Hades within and around you
only legions of demons
crowd you now
compete to take you
to the greedy arms of Thanatos
you look, without hope, for Charon's arrival
at the edge of the silent river

perhaps, he may transport you to a place
where the vicious bearded one
will find you not
where there are red pomegranates
for you, fallen one.

Reluctant Neighbour

Morning neighbour
          silence
Good morning mi neighbour
          loud silence
Good morning my neighbour
          louder silence
A pleasant good morning to you, gentle sir, madam,
                    back turn

It's not my language
not my tone
it seems
my neighbour just
does not want me
for a neighbour
perhaps, my neighbour
just does not want a neighbour,
especially a friendly one like me.

Old Men Dream Dreams

Old men dream dreams
yellowed memories of defiant eels
struggling at the end of fishing lines
busy Saturdays on a restless
fishing boat
long nights with slender young legs
draped over spent bodies
cold beer, steaming cups of black tea
a mother's smothering hugs
the shape and smell of coffins, funeral parlours
the absence of purple
the absence of green
and the confession box
all in one long haunting dream.

The Uncovering of a Mermaid

I watch in awe
the nimble fingers
of my skilful hairdresser
separating strands
of sleek, blonde mane
from the head of a
well-poised mermaid.

I watch in awe
the unceremonial unveiling
of this mermaid
mane by mane
revealing perishing non-mermaid strands
scattered unevenly
across a neglected scalp
covered by opportunistic scales
and then
there was no mermaid
only a woman
with neglected follicles
who had posed as one.

I watch in awe
as the fingers
of my hairdresser
begin the magic all over
and spiky strands join again
with sleek synthetic black mane
restoring the woman to

her mermaid status,
a new mermaid,
with sleek black mane
these days
it seems
a hairdresser must
be a skilful
hair seamstress too.

(Un)wanted Poems

During the reading
I avoided their eyes
after the reading
I avoided their eyes
the poets before me
made them laugh,
now they smiled at me feebly
some seeming to see me
as a mere figure of fun.

Someone muttered garbled words
something about nation language
and yet another mumbled
something about poems
that were too staid and puny
needing a little carnivalesque
and yet another suggested
a little reggae riddim
woulda good yes
I smiled feebly at them
and avoided their probing eyes.

Her Fear of Fear

She fears fear.
she hates the way
it curls up inside of her
and squashes
her very core
she dreads fear
deeply...

Going Back

when I returned
to the place I had carried in my head
for such a long time
I squeezed myself
into the tiny space
chagrined...
somehow I remembered it
differently...

when I was a little girl
it was a vast playing field
now the bench
can hardly hold my books

when I returned
to the place I had carried in my head
for such a long time
complacent dust stirred, tickled my nostrils
cottony cobwebs clouded my vision
I struggled to see in the dark
somehow
I remembered it
differently

when I was a little girl
it was a bright sunny garden
now the rays of the sun
barely penetrate the cloud of gloom
hanging over it
such a funny thing it is...
remembering.

Praying Mantis

praying mantis
camouflaging himself
in my exuberant hibiscus hedge
pretending to pray
but waiting to pounce
on an innocent prey

not at all like a prayer warrior
even if a prayer warrior
sometimes prays for deadly stings
and bites
upon any
who would prey on the weak
the helpless and the praying

praying mantis
devourer of careless creatures
hardly ever pernickety
a silent killer
pretending to pray
in my bountiful hibiscus hedge.

Grief in Hyperbole

when Suzie got news
of Johnny's death
her bones turned to water,
she fell to the ground
and wept blood
that clotted as it fell to the ground
like huge balls of stone

such grief
Miss Jane
had never seen
in her century-long life
and she wept torments of water
for Suzie
for she believed in
grieving for the living.

Reunion Dream

she met him
in the conference room
such a brief encounter
but enough
to disclose
eloquence
erudition
allure
spellbound by
firm handshake
and solid frame
she vowed to meet him again...
that night
she dreamt of such a meeting
once again
in the conference room
the enchantment
suddenly an enigma
as he painted his toenails
with polish the colour of scarlet.

"Free Shampoo"

the neon sign stressed
"Free shampoo for every weave"
imagine...
they would punish me
for wearing my own hair
make me pay for my own shampoo...

but, if I bought the hair of a monk
or a cadaver in India or Brazil
and glued it to my scalp
they would reward me,
I could get my hair washed
with essence of coconut oil,
lime leaf and mint
without paying a cent
imagine that...

Hypotheses

If I lived in a far-away place
they would send a supersonic jet for me
roll out a red and velvet carpet
and enclose me in a circle of love
they would touch my face
tell me my skin is soft
mop the sticky sweat from my brow
with a never before used linen handkerchief
crown me with the colour of orange marigolds
present me with native tokens
and say here
take this
this is the word of our mouths
flesh of our flesh
make it yours
you are part of us now
you are us

write
we will read
speak
we will listen
cover our rocky paths with words
like soft hibiscus petals
paint pictures of beauty
never before imagined
speak any truths you know

if I lived here and left
and came again
they would touch my face
tell me it is beautiful, soft
unusual, striking
they would say speak
inscribe your words
on our hearts and faces
take our words
and transform them with your magical touch
ones you discovered in faraway lands

if I came from far away
they would take me
to the squares, the plazas
where sophisticated old ladies
sit and sip red and white teas
they would take me to the bar
where young intellectuals
sit and debate the politics of inclusiveness
they would at last take me
and say they truly know me.

if I came from far away
or left and returned
they would kiss my ring
read my words
and confess
their undying love.

Real Flowers

when I was a little girl
I often picked golden marigolds
in my neighbour's wide open field
sometimes, early in the morning
when they were still wet with dew
sometimes, at midday
when they glowed in the golden sunlight
morning or midday
I tied them in little bundles
pretended I was a flower girl
and danced to the music in my head
holding them close to my face
pictured myself
carrying them to church
on Harvest Sunday

but always
I ended up
discarding them
with a secret wish
they were daffodils instead
the ones I saw in books
the ones I yearned for
and now
I deeply despise flowers
that only bloom in books.

Eating Words

eventually
you learn
to swallow words
not spit them out
or use them as missiles
but chew them at full tilt
escape, that way, the insipidness
of cynicism and rancour
push them deep, into your gut
let them attach themselves
to the walls of your stomachs
to the villi of your intestines
to die there quietly
eventually.

On the Edge of Hell

I saw the dragon
as I slept,
owner of the bottomless pit
breathing flames of hatred and spite.
I struggled with him
on the edge of the pit
boiling, with the blood of poisonous snakes
I fought with all my might
he, with terror and guile.

I awoke in fear and fright
discovered, I had barely escaped
being thrown into the bottomless pit
boiling, with poisoned blood
I had clung to a halo
that was not even mine.

I Remember

I remember when
my village was the Garden of Eden
we romped and rolled around in the big den
we were all owners
or rather the grown-ups were
we children reaped,
"You can pick anything
except mi mint bush,"
Miss Millie would shout

We picked red, yellow, purple blossoms
from her shoe black bush
marigold and lady slippers
adorned our hair with little bouquets
plucked rose petals and sprinkled them
and frightened shame-ol-ladies,
along our paths.

I remember when
my village was an orchard
we were all planters
or rather, the men and women tended
watered, manure, we children reaped
ate the first, second and third fruits
we bit into their firm skins
succulents, drupes, berries
juice oozing through our fingers
down to our elbows.

"Pick anything except mi Julie Mango,"
Miss Sybil would say
we remembered our manners
thanked her and moved on
to Miss Dill's Star Apples

and I remember when my village
was a playing field
safe, secure, sheltered from evil
we were all innocent
oblivious to harm, and suffering
we all played and the grownups, cheered

we never saw him
lurking in the background
the monster that would change our village
rob us of its Arcadian charm
"careful how you walk through de ball ground,"
Miss Dasa shouts now
as we sit and remember
our village
the way it used to be.

Encounter with a Canadian Border Security Guard

Ma'am, your pre-arranged permit is for two weeks at a University
here no problem here at all you're pre-approved, ma'am.

(nodding his head in approval)

Thank you, I say quietly
after all, I have been waiting in line
for more than two hours
on this pre-approved permit

he continues, oblivious
to my tiredness and impatience
please note you are not allowed to do child care not interested I
say or work in a factory he rambles on not interested I repeat or
work on a farm or work in a hospital or work in a restaurant his
voice is now a hum... I am trying to block it out...
he hands me the permit
Oh, and you are not allowed to work in the sex industry

I take my permit and say
Sir, I am just going to sit in a little corner of a University here and
do nothing nothing at all, to be on the safe side....

Caleb's First Day in Heaven

Hallelujah! Praise God!
I'm gonna walk these streets of Glory now

Heaven pretty fi true,you know
Is de glory of God you know
Shining all aroun, pretty fi true

Ah glad a reach
Tank you Jesus! Hallelujah!

But wait...
Ah who dat?
No Clifton from de Adventist Church...
Adventist people get in here so? Eh eh.

Heaven pretty doan, praise God.
Hold on, me a see right?
No Dawn dat from de Catholic Church in a Liguanea?
Box cover, an look over deh so
De Apostolic man from beside mi Granmadda, alma!
speaking of Grandmadda
a weh she deh ?

She no did seh is ongle people from fe her church comin here
She betta mek sure she roun off de hundred and forty four thousan
it look to me like we near it....

Mi Jesus , me neva know seh
all kinda people would be here
I wonder how I can get a message back to Pastor
fe seh doan preach dat message again

fa all kina people
from all kina church up here
is a whole heap a we gwine come here den
is a mult - dimension and multi - denominational place !
I jus glad I am part of whatever number...

See me Granny dere !
Granny, me reach!
Ah come to walk de streets of Glory wid Jesus!
Ah mek it Granny, ah mek it.
Ah didn't go to your church
But ah mek it Granny, ah mek it.
Praise God ah mek it!

Mama's Handbag

Mothers Make Magic
(For mothers everywhere)

they create magic
mothers do
everyday
they stretch time like endless
elastic ropes
that children swing on
to the moon and back
mothers
make tuneful onomatopoeia
and put the night on hold,
they keep the day running
as their sons float their kites
on the wind,
games must be played,
bodies fed,
fantasies spun
with the thread
of magical words,
songs must be sung,
the stars repainted in the sky
everyone must go to the moon
and back
as mothers make magic.

The First Mother

the first mother did not prick
her fingers picking
red roses for her children or her man
she just ate
the wrong fruit
they say that's how
she hurt herself

the first mother was denied
the chance to mother
it was her fault you say
that's how she robbed herself
and lived the life
of a dried up peach
trying to see life and joy
beyond the restless purple-blue waves
where heaven and earth meet.

Birthing of Sons

Men, all two
they leave a mother's day card
hidden in my handbag.
I read it and smile
reminisce on fourteen hours of travail
to bring forth the first to light
and the voice of
the anaesthetist counting to ten
while I mutter
yeah though I walk
through the valley of the shadow of death
before they plucked
the second one
from my womb
flesh of my flesh
one born in Spring at dawn
the other in the mid-morning Summer's sun.

Strong black men
they will help their country
keep its pride
and take women
through the rites
of bringing men and women
into the world.

Mother Me

I shall be Hannah
staring sterility and loneliness
in the face
while magnifying
the name of the Almighty.
I shall be
the Shunamite woman
never once doubting the God
of the man of Mt. Carmel
ordinary mother that
I am
living on my knees
mostly believing
for my children's sake
redemption
for the children
of my womb
and those of my will
Amen.

Mothers

of every shape and form
question their world
dominated by isms
racism, classism, sexism
mothers speak
and overturn
taboos
probe the Word
authoritative and unbending
persuasive and free.

Mothers speak
words of truth
straightforwardly
and debunk your myths
and hogwash.

Mothers write
personal trajectories
and transform
life.

Last Will and Testament
(for Marc and Zac)

to my two sons, I bequeath you
my words,
firm and pointed
many edged swords
infused with the Word
the spring of all gifts, incomparable,
you will
carry them in your heads
and in your hearts
they'll keep you new every morning
grounded deep
in light and truth.

The Family Firm

my two grandmothers formed
a two-woman firm
and together
they cured all forms of illnesses,
afflictions and maladies
of my cousins, siblings
aunts, uncles,
the whole village

every bruised knee
running nose
running belly
loss of appetite
sore gum
necessitated a trip
to one or the other
for one had the cure
for blood and skin problems,
the other the cure
for eyes, nose and throat
belly and lung problems

their instruments were their eyes
sharp, piercing, probing.
they spun us in all directions
studied our eyes
pressed our ear lobes
poked us in the ribs and cheeks
made their diagnosis

and gave us medicine
from their medicine chests

cool soothing
sticky ointments
green and brown liquids
all created from plants
they pulled from their gardens,
a serious illness
could mean
ginger and lemon grass
or guinea hen weed, cerasee
or tamarind leaves
arrow root or aniseed tea

they had a bush or grass
or leaf for every illness
and when we swallowed
bitter aqueous substances
we doubted not once
that our bellies
would soon feel good
when we gritted our teeth
as stinging crushed leaves
or peppery powder was
spread on our sores
we believed
we would be healed
soon, soon
and when we could run
skip and play hopscotch

we knew that they
had healed us with
magical medicines
from their gardens,

and we believed
that one day we could
be just as they were
doctors with healing potions
but we never learnt their secrets
never had their touch
never studied their plants
and so we tell the story
that they were the
best doctors we
ever knew.

A Mother's Day Flight

it was a reunion
a Mother's Day plan
to meet estranged children
cover the wound with new cloth
stitch the patches with new thread
the anticipation and doubt
the happiness and fear
the longing and hope
the questions without answers
the certainty and uncertainty
too much for a heart
broken many times
by disappointment
the mother collapses on the tarmac
at Vere Bird International Airport
like an over-moist paper bag
and dies
while a repentant son
waits in the arrival lounge
pensively and patiently...

Mama's Handbag

Una bolsa bien usada
its scratched leatherette
not even a poor Louis Vuitton imitation
inside the labyrinth of secret compartments
a chest of quaint surprises
an old, forgotten, half stick
of Wriggley's Spearmint, my favourite
pieces of water crackers
rolled up in crumpled wax paper
leftovers from last week's visit
to the gastroenterologist
a neatly folded silk handkerchief
embroidered with my initials
a sweaty mint ball
sticking to greasy brown paper
a twisted crochet needle
holding a spool of red thread together
my first tooth
or what was left of it, apparently returned
by the tooth fairy
or perhaps was never taken
a button, just like the one

I need for my blue plaid dress
the first Easter card I made
showing Jesus on the cross
singing glory hallelujah.

Mama's dilapidated handbag
preserves the secrets of my life
tells my stories
between its tattered lining.
Mama's prized possessions
keep us close.

The Mother of an Addict

It's my fault, my fault
I pampered him too much,
   even when he was rude,
but I took him to Sunday School
till he was twelve,
   and older
showed him God, the Bible, Jesus on the cross,
taught him
the twelve commandments,
   all twelve,

No, it's his fault,
   his fault,
he is to blame,
   he's twenty-four,
not twelve,
I will not bear blame
that belongs to him,
   no, no, no
but, I still question
is it me who left things
unsaid, undone
or did he forget the things I said?
   so many things,
so many times...

Prayer for Jennifer Pinckney
(June 2015)

If you knew
that this day would come
like this
so swiftly, like a barefaced thief
in the middle of the night
you would speak to widows
like Corretta King, or Jackie Kennedy
or maybe just the lady next door
ask them
how did your belly
carry such grief and pain
how did you look
your young children
in the eyes
answer the questions
asked and unasked?

You would ask them
how do you walk past
a wooden box
encasing the lifeless body of your lover,
your children's father

I pray for you,
for your mother's heart
as you hold your girls
and tell them
of the strong black man

their Daddy is
of how his love for them
did not die
when his body succumbed
to the enemy's bullets
of the many fights he won
before he was cut down
by the enemy's bullets
I pray for you,
for strength that passeth
all understanding
sufficient for you
and for your little girls...

I pray for you.
Amen.

They Did Not Bring Back Our Girls

The world watched
in disbelief,
as an anaemic government reacted,
talked empty talk
mothers wept, fathers fainted
fear walked through the village with the stealth of a thief
two hundred girls
stolen from their beloved village
suffer alone.

Forget Me Not
(For daughters and sons...from any parent)

When I begin to forget
who I am
who you are
where I'm from,
where you are from
will you be there
to remind me?

And when you help me to remember
will you also remember
for my sake, and yours
our best kept secrets and fondest memories,
And will you remember to
smile at the sea for me

Caribbean Global

Awesomesauce!

a Jamaican sprinter being chased
down the tracks in Beijing, London, Rio
a Jamaican hurdler taking gold
a Jamaican student who speaks
Chinese, French and Spanish

Awesomesauce!
Any Gabriel García Márquez paragraph
a Barbadian eating Jamaican jerked pork
and showing it's the only real deal,
a Trinidadian jumping to Jamaican reggae
shouting that it is the music of all music
put calypso to shame
real reggae rhythms,
Awesomesauce!

Caribbean Global

"To be colonized is to be removed from history."
(Walter Rodney)

young St. Lucian artist
making deliberate strokes
paintbrush on white canvas
such *panache*,
the image of the Thames unfolds
revealing a poinciana, flamboyant,
on fire, on a tiny island
in the centre of the sleeping river,
the river flows undisturbed, around it
our young painter paints, with gusto

cool Jamaican bass guitarist
strumming his favourite reggae song
on a stage in Johannesburg
pom _pom _pom _podom _pom ♪
burum _bum _bum _bum _burum _bum _bum ♪
sounds of freedom
on the bass guitar
migration from Kingston, Georgetown, Bridgetown
to London, New York, Amsterdam, Brussels
journeying,
a reminder of home and self

gifted Grenadian student
in the library at the Ivy League University
in New England
writing new identities.

All over the world,
Caribbean people in action
decolonization in progress
Caribbean people
engaging oppositional politics
strumming the bass guitar
laughing othering in the face
writing freedom
strumming reggae songs
bodum, bom _bom _bom _bom _bom _bom ⸢
borum, bom _bom _bom ⸢
claiming space
bom - bom - bom - bom
borum - bom − bom!

The Middle Passage

Yéè ikú àlùmúntu!
Yéè pàrìpà!

the seas rumbled with Yoruba sounds
which the wind whipped
deep into its belly,
betrayed ones groaned,

Ènìyàn abìdì yánáyàán!
those tired of fighting, surrendered,
expressed their sorrow in agonised groans
Yéè
The waves shuddered under
the weight of those sounds
and carried them, back and forth
from the shores of West Africa
over the purple blue waves of the Caribbean Sea
long before dreary boats
struggled into ominous ports
long before the journey
into the heart of terror

the wind carried the echoes
back and forth
Yéè Yéè
sounds that came
from deep in the belly
of starving princes, warriors

village leaders and kings
unaccustomed to restraint
hunger, savagery

it was better to groan
than die without sound
like a tired old man with emphysema
waiting for death
to make its final squeeze
sounds of agony and dying
the only hints of life
in that interminable passage.

When the Yellow Pouis Bloom

the sun
can go to sleep,
rest,
in any corner
of the Caribbean
where yellow pouis
bloom
                spread
their golden feathers
like a million
suns shattered
their golden rays
                scattered
illuminating
every corner
brightening smiles
cooling hot water
evoking dreams
making eyes twinkle with glee
as each petal
glows
a golden yellow
                shimmering
sparkling
like new gold.

Alternative Discourse

Wha a gwan mi dups?

Mi deh ya my yout.

Yuh hear bout di Miggle East ting an ting?

Yu mean di Israeli Palestine ting?

Serious ting dat my yout.

Dat mi a say too.

Babylon business.

True true ting.

Freedom an justice time.

You done know.

Time fi peace.

Peace an love.

Bun out wickednis.

Nuh say nutten.

Compliments of a Jamaican Man

It kinda haad when de only compliments
you get is from a no teet tiad-lookin man,
lookin poorer dan church mouse
on de side a de road
it haad.

Laas week I dress up
in my brand new frock an shoes
I walk pass ten respectable looking man
in jacket an tie
an not one of dem say hi to me,
fool fool an slow, an insecure
but de fus no-teet
gummy mouth man I meet
smile an say, "hi dawlin
I can come home wid you?"

Self-certainty is a Jamaican man, widout teeth
gap wider dan train tunnel
widout money
widout cologne,
calling to you, "hello dawlin,"

I smile, show my thirty-six an say
"no dawlin
you haffi grow teet fus,
...even two
you hear."

Dilemma of a Bandit

the bandit hated his job
said so every day, lamented,
God, you know
I hate this bandit job
hate it bad bad

the look of fright
on the face of that frail woman in the shoe store
and that young fellow last week
just change his first pay cheque
de joy on him face
but him was careless
step outa de bank
wid de fat envelope
in him han
advertising de money
temptation,
yield not to temptation
my mother always say
for yielding is sin
forgive mi sins lawd
but even me
wid my guilty conscience
could not resist
dat oversize envelope.
Ah sorry fi him though
bawl like baby
when I grab dat envelope.
Den de Pastor

wid de church offering
step out big and bold
with him head high
bag in han
like he going
to give communion
I feel it deep deep in my heart
when I kick him and grab de bag
heavy like lead
I could hardly run
one of the challenges of dis job
you lift some real heavy weight.

Poor soul
all now I can hear him
begging de Lord to
"Stop him in his tracks!
He is an angel of darkness
that unholy thief!
angel of darkness!"

Angel of darkness?
Ah was offended to hear him
talk about me
in dat manner
Ah hold on to de bag tight
an run wid all mi might
Ah say, "Tank you dear Gawd,
Ah get wey again!"

But I have to confess
like how sinners confess to priest
I hate dis bandit ting
But what I going to do?
I got to live
I have to do my job
and do it good an proper.

Tony Come Home from Jail Change

Tony come home from jail change,
                walking' roun' boasy
Tony smile,
                feeling nice,
teeth white like coconut milk
Tony stepping like him sweet,
                clicking him heels,
face full a pleat,
                they kinda neat.
Tony moving cool cool
like coconut water
head high like village king
Tony trying to forget
seven hundred and twenty days
a hungry belly
in a two by four cell

Johnny come box him
                blap blap
tell him, I want mi pig,
                him serious,
Tony face red like ackee pod
but Tony turn the other cheek
                and smile sweet.

Bully come slap him
                plaf plaf
I want mi money,
                him very serious,

Uriah shout,
                          like Tony deaf,
I want my money now!
Tony suck him teeth
after seven hundred and twenty days
in hell
rat feeding on him toes
pissing in him face
cockroach poking them way
under him eyelids
and badman jooking knife in him side.

What would phase him now
Johnny demand for pig?
                    Ha!
Uriah fixation on money?
                    Ha! Ha!

his eyes announced without words
I owe no man nothing
I pay everything
in a two by four cell
I never going back to jail.

Human Rights
(for all people)

right to say so and so,
we like to say,
right to do so and apparently so,
some people fight,
to show their rights
are the only rights
that matter
some people fight
to show the rest of us
we should not speak
we should not do
or even be.

Mourning a House

the loss of a house
one you've lived in all your life
is like a miscarriage
losing the child
you have been growing inside of you
for months

you feel the fingers of pain twist deep
inside your abdomen
you feel the sharp teeth
of disappointment and loss
you feel the nausea
caused by interminable regret, remorse
for long-term and short-term dreams unrealized

you remember the corner of the garden
where you planned to grow some red roses, one day
how you planned to paint the kitchen
in your favourite calypso yellow, and how
you meant to trim the mango tree
that shades the back verandah

you flinch from the guilt of abandoning this house
as you would each time
the image of your still-born child
would come to mind...
eventually, you can only grieve in silence

no-one wants to know your grief or pain
so you just keep on smiling at the sea.

One Hundred Years of Literary Indulgence
(For Gabriel García Márquez)

another hundred years,
we who come after
those who came before
and those who follow the ones
after us
and those after them
will read your stories
search the pages
criss-cross of endless words
and short sentences
labyrinth of complex images
painted with your multi-coloured words
for a hundred years and more...

What Google Know

ebryting
it seems
...or so everybody tink
Google say
mi is Jamaican
dat is true
Google say
mi is black
very, very true
me hear say google say
me is a mister
it mus be a internet joke!
me hear say gioogle say
me lie
is mistaken identity dat.
Me hear say google seh
me is dead
(Dead wid laugh).
I woulda like google fi say
is who kill me,
how, when
and where.

Glossary

Èniyàn abìdì yánáyàán – Yoruba expression of deep agony at
the betrayal of a trusted friend.

| yéè pàrìpa!, | – Yoruba expressions used to express
| yéè ikú àlùmúnu | deep grief and agony at the
occurrence of terrible events.

Macca   – Jamaican Creole for thorn.

yéè   – Yoruba expression of pain.

Other Books by Paulette A. Ramsay

- *Afro-Mexican Consructions of Diaspora, Gender, Identity and Nation.* Kingston: UWI Press, 2016.
- *Aunt Jen.* London: Heinemann Caribbean Writers, 2002.
- *Under Basil Leaves.* An Anthology of Poems. London:Hansib Publications, 2010.
- *October Afternoon.* Hansib Publishers, 2012.

Co-authored Books

- *The Afro-Hispanic Reader.* Kingston: Ian Randle Publishers, 2016.
- *Between Two Silences.* Translated Short Stories of Hilma Contreras by Paulette A. Ramsay and Anne-María Bankay. Kingston: Awarak Publishers, 2004.
- *Blooming with the Poius.* A Rhetorical Reader for Caribbean Tertiary Students. Kingston: Ian Randle Publishers, 2008. Co-edited with McLaren, Harding and Cools.
- *Cheveré:* Spanish for Caribbean Secondary Schools. Books 1, 2 and 4. Paulette A. Ramsay et al. Essex, England: Pearson Educational Limited, 2005.
- *Español Avanzado.* Paulette A. Ramsay et al. Kingston: Ian Randle Publishers, 2013.
- *On Friday Night.* Translated novel of Luz Argentina Chiriboga by Paulette A. Ramsay and Anne María Bankay. Kingston: Awarak Publishers, 2008.
- *Practice Papers for CXC Spanish.* Paulette A. Ramsay and Anne-María Bankay. Kingston: LMH Publishers,1998.

CPSIA information can be obtained
at www.ICGtesting.com
Printed in the USA
LVHW020108090819
627063LV00001B/153/P